doll Pets

Teach your doll how to pamper her pets using the supplies and ideas inside!

D1506424

Published by American Girl Publishing
Copyright © 2015 American Girl

Questions or comments? Call 1-800-845-0005,
visit **americangirl.com,** or write to Customer Service,
American Girl, 8400 Fairway Place, Middleton, WI 53562-0497.

Printed in China
15 16 17 18 19 20 21 LEO 10 9 8 7 6 5 4 3 2 1

Editorial Development: Trula Magruder
Art Direction and Design: Sarah Boecher
Production: Jeannette Bailey, Judith Lary, Paula Moon, Kendra Schluter
Photography: Youa Thao, Warren Rader
Craft Styling: Trula Magruder
Set Styling: Casey Hull, Rachel Gremminger, Kim Sphar
Doll Styling: Kelly Erickson, Julia Kinney
Illustrations: Sarah Boecher, Stacey Peterson

Dear Doll Lover,

What do you do if your doll adopts a dog, cat, rabbit, guinea pig, hamster, horse, fish, or other pet? Make it an un*fur*gettable experience with the accessories, activities, and advice inside!

On the very first day, your doll's pet will need all the essentials to eat, sleep, and play. That means a lot of help from you.

From leashes and litter trays to training and tricks—you'll find everything you need in this kit to make your doll's pet adventure a *paw*sitive one!

Your friends at American Girl

Craft with Care

WARNING

Safely tuck your doll and her pets away while you craft so that paint, glue, and other messy supplies don't get on them. Make sure each craft project dries completely before you let your doll or her pet near it.

Keep Your Doll & Pet Safe

When creating doll or pet crafts, remember that dyes from ribbons, felt, beads, cords, fabrics, fleece, and other supplies may bleed onto your doll and pet or their clothes and leave permanent stains. To help prevent this, use lighter colors when possible, and check your doll and her pet often to make sure the colors aren't transferring to their bodies, vinyl, or clothes or the pet's fur. And never get your doll or pet wet! Water and heat greatly increase dye rub-off.

Get Help!

When you see this symbol  in the book, it means that you need an adult to help you with all or a part of the craft. ALWAYS ask for help before continuing.

Ask First

If a craft asks you to use any old item, such as a shirt or sock, always ask an adult for permission before you use it. Your parent might still need it, so check first.

Craft Smart

If a craft instruction says "cut," use scissors. If it says "glue," use craft glue or adhesive dots. And if it says "paint," use a nontoxic acrylic paint. Before you use these supplies, ask an adult to check them over—especially paints and glues. Some crafting supplies are not safe for kids.

Put Up Crafts and Supplies

When you're not using the crafts or art supplies, put them up high or store them away from little kids and real pets. Toddlers and animals might eat your crafts, break them, or even hurt themselves when playing with them.

Pick Out a Pet

If your doll doesn't have a pet, make her one or two!

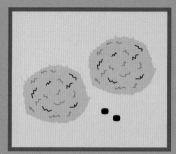

1. Hamster: Glue 2 of the kit's small **pom-poms** together. Let dry. Trim the pom-poms into a hamster shape and size. Glue on **beads** for eyes.

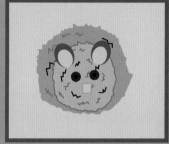

2. Glue on a pink **craft-foam** nose. For ears, cut 2 small circles from brown **felt** and 2 smaller circles from pink felt. Glue these to the head.

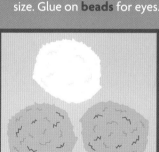

1. Guinea pig: Glue the kit's 2 larger pom-poms together. Let dry. Trim the pom-poms into a guinea-pig shape.

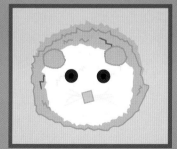

2. To the pet's head, glue a pink craft-foam nose over white **thread** whiskers. Glue on the kit's mini pom-poms for ears. Add bead eyes.

Build a Home

Create cute cages for furry friends and a tiny tank for finned ones.

Happy House

Bring home your doll's hamster or guinea pig in the kit's port-a-pet box, but then make her pet a permanent cage out of colored or clear plastic boxes. Decorate with colored tape, and accessorize with small plastic tubes or boxes. Fill the cage bottom with shredded paper. Don't forget to add an exercise wheel made from a plastic bracelet.

Fish Tank & Carrying Bag

Give your kit's goldfish a fabulous home. Punch out the fish and bring them home using the kit's plastic carrying bags. For a permanent place to stay, look for a small plastic container with a lid. Pour in sand, and add an artificial plant. Decorate the tank with seashell and sea-life stickers. To help the fish "swim," use mini adhesive dots to attach fishing line to each fish, and then attach the line to the underside of the lid.

Pet-Care Book

Cut pieces of scrap paper or cardboard to fill the kit's pet-care book's cover.

Pamper Your Pets

Keep Your Pets Happy & Safe

Dote on Dogs

Collect canine essentials.

Dishes

Create dishes inspired by dogs that love gardens. Decorate mini clay pots with flower stickers, and for a place mat, cover a candy-tin lid with green tape.

Rugs

If your doll's dogs long for a place to rest, cut out floor rugs in appealing shapes. Trace a heart or star pattern on the back of felt or fun fur and cut it out.

Collars

Create dog collars to suit any occasion or outfit. Cut a piece of ribbon that slightly overlaps the pet's neck. Stick one side of a VELCRO® brand mini hook-and-loop fastener dot to the inside end and its mate to the outside opposite end. Decorate the ribbon with stickers, pom-poms, appliqués, or rhinestones.

Leashes

Use an adhesive dot to make a loop on each end of a plastic or fabric cord. Slip a collar through one loop and use the other for your doll's hand. Make sure the leash isn't too long or too short.

Beauty Bed

Make a pup feel warm and welcomed.

1. Look for an embroidery hoop that's larger than the pup. Cut large tulle circles, and squeeze them between the inner and outer hoops.

2. Glue a circle of sparkly felt to cover the top of the hoop. Decorate the rim with ribbon and sequined trim. Place the hoop over a round box.

Kitty Cot

Build a bed for a pussycat to pounce on.

1. Glue gray felt around the rim of a round box lid. Fill the lid with polyester stuffing. Glue a felt circle on top. Trim a mouse-shaped head from a large gray pom-pom.

2. Cut gray and pink felt circles for ears. Glue the ears, bead eyes, plastic-lacing whiskers, a pink pom-pom nose, and a felt tail to the bed. Use ping-pong balls for legs.

Care for a Cat

Fill a room with feline favorites.

Canned Tuna

Glue a small stack of tiny wooden disks together. Wrap the disks with silver duct tape. Cover the tape with the kit's tuna label. Add a silver circle sticker for a pull top if you have one.

Dishes

Serve your cat's pretend tuna in fancy bowls! To make fancy dishes, wrap gold duct tape around the rims of vending-machine capsules. Punch out glitter paper for place mats.

Cat Grass

Wrap green plastic cord into long, loose loops around your hand. Remove the loops, wrap a rubber band tightly around one end, and then snip the loops at the other end. Slip the banded end inside a mini terracotta pot. Finish the pot with the kit's cat-grass label.

Litter Box

Put together the litter box following the kit's instructions. Place the litter box where your doll's cat has easy access to it.

Create Animal Apartments

If your doll adopts a caboodle of critters, build each one a condo.

Condos: Look for a photo/craft box for each pet—a collection of shoe boxes will work, too. (Keep the lids if you want to store the condos later.) Stack the boxes, or place them side by side. If you like, you can attach them with binder clips. Use the kit's mini apartment and decor for a small animal.

Themes: Choose a theme to suit the personality of each of your doll's pets. Then pick the wallpaper, carpets, and accessories to fit that theme.

Walls: To cover the walls inside each box, use double-stick tape to attach scrapbook paper, glitter paper, wrapping paper, place mats—anything that will stick to the walls.

Floors: For flooring, choose faux fur, felt, textured fabric, tape, or even pom-poms. Attach the carpets with double-stick tape or glue.

Decor: To decorate, look for miniatures, small toys, stickers, stuffed mittens, 3-D scrapbook accents, or anything else that fits the condo's theme. Don't fill the condo with too much stuff, though, or you won't have room for your doll's pet!

Build a Show-Horse Stall

Give a special horse a place to relax and reflect on wins.

Stall

Look for a cardboard box to fit your horse. Using the kit's barn-wood paper, make enough color copies to cover the box, or just color the box to look like barn wood. If your box has a large opening, keep the horse inside the stall by adding a thin balsa-wood strip to span the gap. Use brown and black watercolor paints to "age" the wood. Let dry, and then glue the wood strip to the box on each side of the opening.

Hay Bales & Feed Bag

Spread a little hay, shredded paper, or raffia on the stall floor—or glue "hay" scrapbook paper to the inside lower edge of the box if you like. You can find miniature hay bales at craft stores. For a feed bag, stuff a small plain bag, seal it, and attach one of the kit's feed stickers.

Ribbons & Reins

Create horse-show awards from punched paper and ribbon, or use the kit's awards. For reins and other tack, attach a decorative hook to the side of the stall, and hang leather laces, silver ribbon, or a silver bracelet.

Dress for Winter

Keep pets warm on cold days.

Hoodie, Turtleneck & Jacket

✋ Ask an adult before using any items suggested on this page. For a hoodie, slip a kneesock on the pet so that the heel is behind the head. Lightly mark the sock at the pet's nose, remove the sock, and cut a slit at the mark for the face. Slip the sock on again, mark the front paws and tail, remove the sock, and cut a slit at each mark. For a turtleneck sweater, cut the leg off a kneesock. Slip the sock on so that the cut edge is at the feet. Fold up the cuff. For a jacket, cut the sleeve off an infant bunting coat, and place the hand opening at the pet's face. Trim the sleeve to fit, and decorate.

Fleece Sweater & Cap

For a sweater, slip a fleece sock on a pet so that the cuff is at the neck. Lightly mark the sock at each paw, the tail, and the rear. Remove the sock, and cut a small slit at each mark. Trim the sock to just cover the rear. Glue a rear seam, and let dry. For a cap, slip another fleece sock on the pet's head. Gather the heel fabric and extra fleece, and tie them into a knot. Trim to the knot end. Accent with a sticker.

Knitted Hat & Boots

For a hat, cut the cuff off a glove. Glue a ponytail holder to the uncut bottom edge, and tie at the top. Add a sticker accent. For boots, snip the fingers off the glove. Cut a sole from craft foam, and glue it to the boot. Accent with a ponytail holder.

Groom Your Pet

Pamper pets before showy events.

Displays, Decor & Wares

A plastic bin makes a great counter to display your wares. Add a craft-foam top. Display infant washcloths, craft-foam soaps, and hair products (made by attaching the kit's labels to small sticky notepads). For slippers, trace a paw on craft foam twice, and cut out the pieces. Glue a faux-fur strip between the foam layers. Repeat for each slipper. Decorate the spa with precut felt pieces for rugs, and post the kit's spa signs. For spa gifts to customers, use adhesive dots to attach the kit's ties or bow ties to the pets' collars.

Robe, Wrap & Slippers

For a robe, ask an adult if you can use a pair of fleece socks. Cut off the feet. Slip a sock top onto one side of the pet with the finished edge at the neck. Repeat with a second sock top on the other side. Cut a belt from leftover fleece. For a hair towel, slip the heel of a sock on the pet's head, gather the extra fleece at the top, and tie a knot. For spa booties, ask an adult if you can cut the fingers from a glove.

Tub, Dryer & Treatment

For a tub, place the pet in an oval container, and cover it with polyester stuffing. Raise the tub to doll level. For a dryer, seat the pet under an adjustable lamp—but **never** plug it in! For a treatment, tie a stretchy cord around the pet's head, and attach the kit's cucumber slices to the cord with adhesive dots.

19

Pose for a Show

Your doll can strut her pup's stuffing.

Outfits

Ask an adult if you can use old dresses, socks, and place mats for these gowns. **Red:** Slip a decorative sock on the dog. Lightly mark the paws and tail, remove the sock, snip each mark, and put the sock back on. Then cut the center from a red place mat for a hat. Add ear holes and a bow. Next, cut a section of the leftover place mat for a skirt. Glue a ribbon to the skirt's waist, let dry, and tie the skirt around the dog. **Fancy:** Slip a dress sleeve on the pet so that a fancy cuff is at the neck. Mark the paws and tail as described earlier. Keep the sleeve long in back for a train. Remove any fancy trimming from the other cuff, and glue the trim to the train. **Sky:** Slip the dog into a dress sleeve so that a pretty cuff is at the neck. Mark and cut holes for the front legs and tail. Fold the extra fabric over the rump for a bustle. Decorate with silk flowers. **Dottie:** Slip a stretchy sock over the pet so that the heel is on the back of the head and the cuff is around the legs. Mark the dog's nose and tail, remove the sock, snip each mark, and put the sock back on. Gather the extra fabric at the head, and tie it off. Cut the gathered fabric into strips. Tie a bead on each strip.

Crowd

Use the kit's audience poster to create a crowd to watch the dogs in action.

Train for the Agility Course

Now your doll can put her pet through her paces!

Equipment

Jump Ring: Clip a clothespin to the outer ring of an embroidery hoop. **Weave Set:** Slip straws into an object that will stand upright, such as party horns. Tape the straws upright if needed. Glue or tape the kit's flags to the straws at the top. **Teeter-totter:** For the plank, cover a piece of foam board or cardboard with scrapbook paper. Trim the edges with tape. Place the plank on a small flat object. **Tunnel:** You will need two embroidery hoops big enough for your dog to fit through. Cut a piece of fabric to fit perfectly around the inside hoops and as long as you'd like the tunnel to be. Use adhesive dots to attach the fabric to the inside edge of both hoops. If the tunnel sags too much, slip the larger outside ring inside through the seams. Place the tunnel so that the seam faces the ground. **Hurdles:** Clip drinking straws to clothespins.

Awards

Cut two 3-inch ribbon strips in one color and two in a different color. Place an adhesive dot in the center of each ribbon, and fold both ends to the glue. Crisscross two folded ribbons, and glue them to the back of the awards in your kit. Add hanging ribbons.

Enter a Parade

Create silly and surprising costumes for a pet parade!

Costumes

Ask an adult before using any of the items suggested below. **Kitty:** Tie an elastic band into a loop that will fit around a dog's face. Use an adhesive dot to attach a cat-face appliqué to the elastic. Finish with a ball of yarn and a glove's finger for a tail. **Athlete:** Slip your doll's sporty jacket on her pet, and then stuff the arms. Add a 3-D foam-finger sticker to each cuff. Slip a pair of your doll's sneakers on the pet's front paws. Attach ribbon to punched paper circles for medals. **Bunny:** Cut two fingers off a white glove. Attach pink craft foam to the fingers for the inner ears. Slip the fingers over the pet's ears. Add a cotton-ball tail. **Ball and Doll:** If a stuffed toy or doll gets damaged or wears out, figure out how the toy will fit on the pet. You may need to snip seams, remove stuffing, or enhance with accessories. **Monster:** A punctured soft rubbery toy or two will make a funny costume if you stretch one over a pet. **Masks:** Attach a mask from the kit to an elastic band. Finish the pet costume with your own ideas if you like. **Unicorn:** Cover a pet with an old white fleece sock. Lightly mark the pet's eyes, nose/mouth, and forehead on the sock, and then remove it. Snip holes for the eyes and nose/mouth, and glue a spiral seashell to the forehead. Gather and tie white yarn strips for a mane and tail.

24

Teach a New Dog an Old Trick

Your doll can wow her friends with these canine commands.

Tricks

Clicker: Give your doll a clicker so that she can train her pet to respond to each click. To make one, glue a miniature clothespin to a narrow piece of cardboard or balsa wood. Let dry, and then snap the clothespin to make a sound. **Respond:** Pull out one of the kit's dog bones, and leave it on the dog's nose until she hears a click. **Shake:** Help your doll hold her dog's paw in her hand to shake. **Retrieve:** Pull out the kit's mini mail or newspaper, and set it out for your pet to fetch. **Jump Up:** Balance your doll on her hands and feet, and then help the dog jump up on her owner's back. **Catch:** Your doll can play with her dog with a flying disk (found at party stores).

Bad Dog!

If pets are caught in the act, your doll should be firm but forgiving.

Torn Chair

Cut a piece of fabric large enough to cover your doll's favorite chair. Remove the fabric, make a few tears, and then tape the fabric to the chair back and bottom. Slip polyester stuffing under the tears so that it looks like the chair's stuffing is bursting out.

Unrolled Toilet Paper

Cut a strip of toilet paper or tissue paper to wrap around the cardboard spool of an empty cellophane tape holder. Spread more TP around your doll's room.

Ripped Stuffed Animal

Slip polyester stuffing in a finger puppet. It'll look like the dog has ripped apart a stuffed animal.

Chewed Shoes

Use the doll sole pattern in your kit to make shoes. Trace the pattern twice on craft foam for each shoe, and then glue a strip of fabric between the soles. Let dry, and then rip one up!

Warning: Keep polyester stuffing up and away from all real pets and small children!

Share the Love

Dazzle your doll and her pet with matching dresses and accessories.

Dress

⭐ Ask a parent if you can use a pair of kneesocks. Cut the foot off each sock, and slip the top portion on your doll and on the dog. (See page 16 to learn how to make holes for the dog's feet and tail.) Add an appliqué to the front of each dress. For each skirt, make a loop from an elastic band that will fit around the waist. Tie narrow strips of tulle in any length to fill the bands. Slip on the skirts, and trim the length if needed.

Accessories

For a hair accessory, wrap a piece of tulle around the doll's head, and tie a knot in back. Attach an appliqué if you like. Repeat for the dog.

Send it in!

How does your doll show her pet she cares? To tell us, write to:

Doll Pets **Editor**
American Girl
8400 Fairway Place
Middleton, WI 53562

Sorry, but photos can't be returned. All comments and suggestions received by American Girl may be used without compensation or acknowledgment.

Here are some other American Girl books you might like: